10 THINGS TO FORGET

To be creatively free

DARA GIRARD

To all the artists who have provided me with inspiration.

CONTENTS

Introduction	vii
1. Forget Being Original	1
2. Forget Competition	5
3. Forget an Audience	13
4. Forget Perfection	19
5. Forget Following the Crowd	23
6. Forget the Drama	29
7. Forget Having it Made	39
8. Forget Being Found	45
9. Forget Creating a Masterpiece	51
10. Forget Choosing Sides	57
Sneak Peek	61
Defining Success	63
Also Available	81
About the Author	83

10 Things To Forget: To Be Creatively Free

Copyright © 2015 Sadé Odubiyi

ISBN 13: 978-1949764574

Published by ILORI Press Books

Cover Design and Layout Copyright © 2015 ILORI Press Books

Cover design by ILORI Press Books

Cover Image Copyright © M. Odubiyi

All rights reserved. No part of this publication may be reproduced, stored in a retrieval system, or transmitted in any form or by any means, electronic, mechanical, recording or otherwise, without the prior written permission of the author.

DISCLAIMER

This book is not intended to provide professional advice and is sold with the understanding that the publisher and the author are not liable for the misconception or misuse of the information provided. The author and ILORI Press Books, LLC shall have neither liability nor responsibility to any person or entity with respect to any loss, damage, or injury caused or alleged to be caused directly or indirectly by the information provided in this book or the use of any products mentioned.

ILORI Press Books, LLC

PO Box #10332

Silver Spring, MD 20914

INTRODUCTION

For some reason many aspiring artists (whether a musician, visual artist, writer etc...) want rules. Lots of rules. They want to know whether or not they should use one technology over another. They wonder what their industry gatekeepers (i.e. music executives, agents, editors, gallery owners) are looking for. What's the latest trend? Should they create early in the morning or late at night? Should they go the traditional route or an independent one?

They think that reading about how successful working artists schedule their time, or do their routine—pen versus laptop versus dictation; jam session or independent study—is the key to the castle of success. They couldn't be more wrong.

I've been a working artist for over a decade and I've been able to survive a lot of the hits most working artists face. And I've been fortunate enough to mingle with people who have been in the industry for twenty to forty years (that's one benefit of sticking to a dream, you'll get to meet some of your heroes).

It's a thrilling and humbling experience to meet and talk with these individuals because I discovered they all have two things in common: A bold, fearless joy for the art of their craft *and* business savvy.

Yes, you heard me—business savvy, a topic that is rarely, if ever, spoken about much in the creative world because it's only supposed to be about The Art.

Cue in the laughter.

Long-term professionals know this is a myth fed to neophytes.

Once you hit a certain level, your focus will no longer be to 'just create the best book, song, or software you can'; your job will be to continue to learn and grow your business. The savvy working artists I've had a chance to meet know this. They have dealt with career blows, disappointments and financial hardships. But they're still here and so am I.

Why?

That's what this book is about.

We live in an information age where people think the

more you know, the better you'll be. More often than not, too much knowledge can get in your way. It will make you question yourself. As a working artist, you already know a lot more than you think. You're just afraid you don't.

"To know the road ahead, ask those coming back."

— CHINESE PROVERB

Why?

USA Today bestselling author Dean Wesley Smith calls it the Critical Brain. Author Steven Pressfield calls it Resistance.

It's the primal lizard brain. It's the voice of fear and it will stop your creativity. That's its job. It wants to keep you safe.

But safety is the death of art.

Following a known trend 'just because' is like setting up a lemonade stand right next to three other lemonade stands because it's hot and you want to make pocket change. Why should I choose you when I can get the very same thing from the kid next to you?

But what if you made your lemonade green? Hmmm....

Standing out. That's a scary concept. But if you think of notable artists in any field, there's usually something about their work that sets them apart.

These notable, working artists put in that little extra that usually gets overlooked. That little extra is what makes all the difference to the long-term working artist who creates with joy for decades.

In order to achieve this you will need to be creatively free.

I hope that the ten things to forget listed in this book will help free you so that you won't be on a conveyer belt of also-rans. So you won't become one of those artists whose work starts to sound the same or who becomes bitter and angry because you believe the industry is harsh to your creations.

You can become the fiercest advocate for your work.

Not in a bombastic way, because if you're a true advocate, you won't have to speak at all. We'll see your work, it will be available and we'll know what you stand for. You'll be one of those working artists who loves what she does. Who wakes up with purpose and passion. Who continues to learn how to grow without losing your special voice.

That's the balance.

Long-term working artists are always learning something new and know how to apply what they learn to themselves. Being a sponge is about as dangerous as being a doormat. People will use you and wring you out.

However, all artists are different so don't follow anything that doesn't suit you.

But...

If you're struggling through creative blocks and unhappiness then I hope forgetting the following ten things will set your genius free.

1
FORGET BEING ORIGINAL

"I could never do that, it's been done before."

"Stories like that have been done to death, nobody reads that anymore."

"I want to be original. I don't want to be second best."

Statements like these have killed wonderful projects before they've even had a chance to flower. Searching for being original makes you believe that everything that comes from your mind must 'wow' the world. It must be something that's never been seen, heard or experienced before. You must be original is a myth.

Here's the secret.

If you just start, your version will be original. You already see the world in an original way. Think of how many people have taken the boy meets girl, or man goes on quest theme and turned them into completely different stories.

> *"Keep in mind that the person to write for is yourself. Tell the story that you most desperately want to read."*
>
> — SUSAN ISAACS

Van Gogh painted flowers totally different than Georgia O'Keefe. The moment you're born the die has been cast—you're original.

You're the mix that spices any project if you're bold enough to be authentically you.

It's like adding something to water. Give five people a glass of water and then give each of them a different food coloring to add to their glass. Although it's just water their glasses will all look vastly different.

Ah, but they will all taste the same.

Okay, but what if someone added lemon, another added strawberries, and one added fizz?

Am I starting to make my point?

They all started with the exact same thing, but what they added made the difference.

It doesn't matter what you start with, it's what you add.

And what successful, working artists add is passion.

They create projects because they want to, because it fuels them. And that's how you can stay productive. Create for fun.

HOW TO FORGET ABOUT BEING ORIGINAL

Just say what you want to say how you want to say it. Ever stopped yourself from saying 'hello?' because it's been said a million times before? Have you ever asked someone 'How are you?' and meant it? Have you ever asked someone 'How are you?' and not meant it? The words haven't changed, but your intention did and that's what originality is all about.

Stop judging your work.

Realize originality doesn't exist in the way you think. Everything comes from something else.

Find another career. Seriously, if you can't get past this myth you're in deep trouble and your working days are numbered. The book *Steal Like an Artist* by Austin Kleon may help.

Remember that your ego will always try to take over.

The only way to free yourself will be to get started. Yes, it's scary to write the first line, paint the first stroke, but the only path to genius is doing the work not letting it get buried under a false objective.

We don't have to connive, cajole or persuade we just have to create with passion. Because focusing on being original leads us to the next trap—competition.

> *"Creativity is the quality that you bring to the activity you are doing.*
>
> *It is an attitude, an inner approach—how you look at things."*
>
> — OSLO

2
FORGET COMPETITION

Artists can learn a lot from athletes.

They can learn the importance of a healthy regime and keeping your body in peak performance. If you want to be a long-term working artist you must treat your body well or you won't last.

Focus on finding time to create, to play and to learn, eat right and sit right (especially if you're a writer). Get a good chair, move every hour, keep your joints limber or your body will betray you in later years. Get enough sleep. Those are excellent ways to make your life pain-free and fun.

The one difference between you and an athlete?

You don't need to compete with others.

It's a silly mindset when aspiring artists stop creating

something because 'it's already been done'. Really? That's your excuse? So are you telling me that once you read a story about a man who reconciled with his father along an Oklahoma trail you'll never read another like it? You heard a band fuse rock and jazz so that's all there is to it? Digital art has reached its peak?

I don't know about you, but there's not enough music, art, or books to satisfy me. Just because I like one singer, artist, or actress doesn't stop me from appreciating—and buying—another. I was one of those kids who, when I first read *Where The Wild Things Are*, said 'read it again' and then when I discovered other authors who could write about different worlds, I devoured them. I didn't read one author and then say, "That's it! I'm completely satisfied. I don't need to read any other authors." I went looking for more.

Artists can't create fast enough to keep consumers satiated. Even if a novelist wrote a book every month, his weeks, months—dare I say years—of work can be devoured in just a few hours or days. Readers always find time to read someone else, as well as their favorite authors. That's why there are those lists 'If you like so and so you may also like...'

Marketers want artists to believe that the projects we're creating are interchangeable widgets. In publishing, they'll tell writers that statistics show that

4,500 books are created every day and they're all competing with your work.

Um…no.

A book about chicken farming won't compete for my attention because I'll never read it. But if I do…I'd be interested in the small chicken farmer. Not the industrial one, but the one who's owned a farm for generations. Or maybe the guy who gave up a job on Wall Street to try something new like organic farming.

Or maybe I only want to know about chicken farming in Wales.

When it comes to music, a listener may be in the mood for Japanese funk one day and country the next. And not just *any* country, they want hard rock not folk.

Art is specific. So are consumers.

> *"If fame happens, good. If it doesn't happen, good. It should not be the consideration. The consideration should be that you are enjoying whatsoever you are doing. It is your love affair."*
>
> — OSHO

Competition puts the artist in the wrong mindset and produces three dangerous outcomes:

It can kill the joy of discovery. When you see other artists as the competition, how can you enjoy their work? You'll soon become one of those annoying pseudo-artists who criticizes everything but creates nothing. You know the type. They can't listen to music because everything out there sucks. They don't read because all books published today are trash. They don't go to museums because they already know what all the great artists accomplished and nobody living can match them.

> *"Do not waste the remainder of thy life on thoughts about what other people are doing."*
>
> — MARCUS AURELIUS

Artists need to experience life to the fullest and that means seeing and admiring someone else's brilliance.

Let yourself indulge in a book that gives you goose bumps, listen to a song that makes your heart sing, taste a meal that makes your lips tremble in memory.

When you can appreciate others with an open heart and mind, then the world opens up and you can be inspired. Soak up the arts, they're your fuel. When you stop reading, listening, seeing, enjoying, your engine will die and so will your career.

You'll lose your confidence. On the flip side some artists are afraid to be exposed to others because they fear they'll never be that good.

Relax. You won't be as good as they are. You're not meant to be them. You are you. When you're no longer in competition you realize it's not a race and there are no winners or losers. You do your thing and let the world follow suit.

It limits your scope. One of the best parts of being an artist is that you get to watch lots of movies, listen to tons of songs, read all the books you want to. It's part of your career. What others do for leisure, is part of your job. Thinking about competition can take this away.

Scarcity is a mindset that has nothing to do with creativity.

There are plenty of ideas, plenty of money, plenty of consumers. No one can diminish your audience.

Remember, to have a long, successful career you don't need everybody to like your work, you just need somebody.

When you take competition out of the mix, your creative scope opens up. Think about how many musicians collaborate. By mixing a genre with another, an artist can expose her work to a completely new audience and help keep the work alive and fresh. And keep the artist alive and fresh too.

Remember, someone else's success doesn't make your path harder. (I know that at times it may seem that way.)

There will always be those artists who appear to be the chosen few who are seen as extraordinary. Sorry, but that has nothing to do with you. They have not taken what should have been yours. They have not drained the pool of consumers who would have bought your work. They just did their job and did it well.

No, I will not discuss quality here because my premise is simple. As Stephen King said,

"If you wrote something for which someone sent you a check, if you cashed the check and it didn't bounce, and if you then paid the electric bill with the money, I consider you talented." (*Everything You*

Need to Know About Writing Successfully—In Ten Minutes)

Yes, it's that simple. If you can convince people to *pay* you for your work, you're talented. That's it.

That's why the long-term working artists who critics continue to pan (and others whose names you've never even heard of) are still out there creating art, entertaining their audience and making a great living.

And that's the point. Your job is to get paid to do the work you love. The moment you start looking outside yourself, focusing on those you think are in competition with you and imagining them racing past to get the gold ring—fame, fortune, awards—you're already losing.

You're losing your own joy of creation.

You're losing the possibility of having fun.

You're wasting time on something that's not important.

HOW TO FORGET ABOUT COMPETITION

Focus on your next project.

Study and admire other artists, but never compare yourself to them.

Focus on competing against yourself.

How are you improving?

What are you doing to make sure you're better this year than you were last year?

Competition in the arts is for suckers. People who think like this are the ones who will get swayed by scam artists who will promise to make them stars. They'll devalue their work for short term success, they'll do whatever it takes to make a lot of money—fast. If this is you, that's fine.

Your short term goals will suit your short-term career.

But if you want a loyal following, a group eager for your next project and a career that sustains you for decades then forget about competition and the next group you imagine looking over your shoulder...

3
FORGET AN AUDIENCE

I know, I know.

You're wondering how can you forget about something that you don't even have?

That may be true, but if you're thinking about what your mother or best friend will say about your work, you already have an audience.

If you're writing to impress an agent or editor, you have an audience.

If you're worrying about what this group of listeners wants versus that group, you have an audience.

If you're afraid of what your friends will think of your mural design, you have an audience.

And thinking about that audience can squash you.

> "Don't think. Thinking is the enemy of creativity. It's self-conscious, and anything self-conscious is lousy. You can't try to do things. You simply must do things."
>
> — RAY BRADBURY

How?

Anything that takes you out of the creative project and has you looking over your shoulder, needs to be forgotten, dismissed, kicked into the corner and starved. Only *you* matter in your creative space. The fearless you.

Many new and aspiring artists haven't given themselves permission to meet this version of themselves. They're too busy trying to create in a certain way, worrying about whether they're a true artist or not.

Do they really have what it takes? they wonder.

Will they make a fool of themselves?

What will others think?

Sorry, forget about an audience and just create.

Trust your instincts.

When you stop thinking and let your bold, subconscious self take the reins, then you'll see your work become something your conscious, rational thinking self would never have allowed you to create.

Okay, here's another secret.

Ever wonder how some artists can be so productive and prolific?

Because they know how to have fun.

They know how to play. If you can keep the spirit of play in your work, you'll never grow tired.

This is not a truth many artists will admit to in public because we've all been taught that the process of creation must remain mysterious and there are certain accepted truths that must be maintained. So to others you can speak about how much work it takes—how hard it is to write your novel, to paint that watercolor, to choreograph that scene, but never believe it yourself.

Being paid to play is the artist's job.

Not to follow boring rules.

Not to meet each day with dread.

Not to listen to the 'Voice of Authority'.

We—the consumer—will not pay you for your doubts, the music you won't share, the book you won't write, or the paintings you won't show.

When should you think about an audience?

After the work is finished.

When you set your artist hat aside and become the businessperson, then you worry about sales and marketing.

Never before.

HOW TO FORGET AN AUDIENCE

Start with joy. You don't have to do the boring and hard part first. Jump into the part that interests you. You don't have to create in any particular order. If you're a writer, write only the scenes that interest you no matter where they happen in the story. Trust me, this works. If you're writing scenes you find boring and tedious, the reader will feel the same. The story will come together, trust your instincts.

If you're a musician don't wait for the right hook, let the hook choose you. Play the one that excites.

Follow your passions. Only focus on production and what you want to express. How much have you gotten done today needs to matter more than 'what will X think?'

Play. Make creating a game.

Remember, people don't know what they want until they see, hear, taste or experience it.

Your job is to create. And keep creating. You'll find an audience. Whatever stops you from doing that is wrong.

Remember, your rational, critical self wants to stop you.

Don't let it.

Are you delighted by what you're working on? Frightened? Surprised? Bored? You're the only one who counts. Have fun. And if you do, you won't get caught up on the next thing to forget...perfection.

> *"You can sit there, tense and worried, freezing the creative energies, or you can start writing something. It doesn't matter what. In five or ten minutes, the imagination will heat, the tightness will fade, and a certain spirit and rhythm will take over."*
>
> — LEONARD BERNSTEIN

4
FORGET PERFECTION

It's not going to be perfect.

So relax and have fun. Perfection is deadly to the creative person because it's as conniving as flattery. They're both lies that sound good.

Perfection is not about striving for excellence or going the extra mile. No, perfection tends to halt you in your tracks. Instead of an open window of possibilities, it's a brick wall. It's the voice that will make you rewrite a scene until the scene becomes pabulum, or make you polish a project until you've rubbed out all its beauty. It's the voice that tells you 'it's not good enough and never will be.'

Perfection is the weapon of the Ego.

It's putting yourself in front of your work, like a stage

momma saying 'That's my baby up there!" You are not your work. It comes through you, that's all. You need to get your ego out of the way.

All great works are wonderfully imperfect. Many artists people now revere had critics and for some they thought their most brilliant work had flaws. But thankfully they continued.

Here's the truth.

As humans, we're not seeking perfection, we're seeking connection. Tell me a story that moves me, intrigues me, write a song that delights me, draw something that informs me. I don't care how, just do it.

Will everyone like it?

Wrong question. Don't ask that.

Do I like it?

Good question. If yes, then do it.

When you are too self-conscious, you lose your power.

Create from your subconscious self. The self few artists can—or want to—explain.

The place where genius comes from.

In this place you don't care what others think, say or do. You're having too much fun. You're in flow, time falls away.

HOW TO FORGET ABOUT PERFECTION

Be imperfect on purpose.

Make doing more important than being. Perfection's close cousin is procrastination and she's clever. She makes you talk about your art, think about your art, but she never lets you do it. Doing it kills her, but you have to be vicious and slay her. Get things done.

Trust yourself. You know the difference between sloppy work and doing your best. Your best always matters.

Give yourself a short deadline. Decide to write a novel in a month, create three songs in an hour, finish a painting in a day, or illustrate a twenty-four-page comic book in twenty-four hours. This won't give you time to worry about perfection.

Will the end product be any good?

Will anyone like it?

Again, wrong questions.

Remember you're not creating for everyone. Create what you want, make it available for those who will appreciate it then work on your next project.

And once you clearly understand this you won't fall into the next trap...

5

FORGET FOLLOWING THE CROWD

"Fashion is about dressing according to what's fashionable. Style is more about being yourself."

— OSCAR DE LA RENTA

By now you know where I'm going with this 'forget it' theme, right?

In order for your creative well to keep refilling, you must make sure that everything you create reflects what you care about. And you have to have the courage to dance to your own beat.

So forget about following the crowd, a hot trend, or whatever external motivation is tossed at you.

Following is not an artist's job—take the reins and lead.

I don't know about you, but I became a freelancer so that I don't have a boss telling me what to

do, what to think, how to behave. I get to choose what my next project will be and it's liberating.

Don't let others take that choice away from you.

No, everything you create will not be adored or make a fortune, but if adoration and money are all you care about there are plenty of other ways to get them. But if you want to be a unique, working artist then don't be like someone else.

Is it scary?

Yes, it can be.

Is it easy? No, but the life of an artist has always involved risk. It's the price you pay for your freedom.

Is it tempting? Absolutely.

Especially when you see others succeeding. Then you may start to wonder about taking short cuts (gaming the system, thinking commerce over creativity).

You'll likely be successful in the short term and if that's your aim, fine.

But if you want to last for decades, it's going to be a painful fall when the crowd turns, the trend cools and you've spent your energy doing something you didn't really like doing in the first place.

Your job isn't to create replaceable widgets.

What do I mean?

You have to be you (yes, I'll keep repeating this because it's important). It may be a harder road if your work is out of step with a current trend or cultural norm, but that's okay. It took comedian Steve Martin ten years to hone his unique, innovative act that would launch him into stardom and a legendary career.

> "Nobody ever takes note of [my advice], because it's not the answer they wanted to hear. What they want to hear is 'Here's how you get an agent, here's how you write a script,'...but I always say, 'Be so good they can't ignore you.'"
>
> — STEVE MARTIN

HOW TO FORGET ABOUT FOLLOWING THE CROWD

Jump in. Don't look back or to the sides, just look forward.

Focus on what you love, others will love you for it.

Ignore the haters, they don't matter. Really. They talk a lot and hurt your feelings, but they don't pay the rent so ignore them. Universal adoration doesn't exist.

Don't let anyone tell you what you should or shouldn't do. They can make suggestions, but they can't dictate.

The real dangerous ones will try to shame you into submission. They'll make seemingly harmless statements like, 'a real [fill in the blank] would do this', or 'who do you think you are?' or 'you'd be a lot more successful if you did [fill in the blank]'. Only listen if you want to, otherwise block them out.

Find inspiration by learning about others who created their own path.

Understand why you're an artist.

Define success for yourself, not to anyone else's standards.

People don't want safe artists who are afraid to say what they feel or think. Who are afraid to be authentically themselves.

Please don't misunderstand me. Causing a ruckus

because that's what you think an artist should do, isn't being artistic.

Being contrary for the sake of attention, is not being artistic.

No, be loud and bombastic or flamboyant and dazzling, if that's really you.

Or be quiet.

It doesn't matter as long as you're genuine.

But forget about following the crowd because that can lead to...

6
FORGET THE DRAMA

My daily schedule is remarkably routine. There are no traumas. Nothing that would interest someone bored enough to write about me. I have a simple lifestyle and keep the drama on the page where it belongs, not in my life.

What does drama look like?

Drink and Drugs

The drug addled, drunken creative looks great on the screen, but rarely lasts long in real life. I've been disheartened by how this myth lures every generation. When I was in my teens, I was friends with a fellow artist who was adamant that the creative mind wasn't truly free unless it was altered by an artificial stimulant.

> *"First you take a drink, then the drink takes a drink, then the drink takes you."*
>
> — F. SCOTT FITZGERALD

It sounds romantic. It sounds cool. It makes a great story, but it's a hell of a life to live.

Many people don't have the right mindset for a freelance career. The instability can be crushing, so don't add to it by being unstable yourself. It's like flying in a plane with a drunk pilot, you're already in a risky situation and now you've made it a hundred times worse. You need to be mentally fit for a long-term career in the arts.

Most working artists I've met are wonderfully ordinary.

They have their family and friends and love what they do.

These artists aren't sniffing white powder up their nose, getting a fix through a needle in their arm, popping pills or drinking bottles of vodka. They are professionals.

Drinking excessively and doing drugs won't allow

you to be yourself. In order to be creatively free and bold, you have to be sober and be able to own your work.

Trouble

Trouble always gets in the way of creativity because it puts the focus on anything but creating.

Trouble is: Always being late for paying gigs, missing deadlines, dating or marrying a person who causes you grief (i.e. sleeps around, hurts you, belittles you etc...), getting ill a lot, picking fights (both online and off), making bad choices (i.e. sleeping with your boss's underage son, buying new clothes instead of paying your rent). Yes, misery loves company and the more misery you have the more attention you'll get. But you won't get anything done.

Working artists don't make room for trouble. It may stop by, but it should never have a place to stay.

Being a starving artist

Initially it will be hard to make a living as a freelance artist.

You may have a lot of false starts--returning to a paying job just to get by and moments living on a shoestring. Early in my career, I used to joke about being a starving artist because it was acceptable and garnered my parents some sympathy, but I knew I wasn't going to stay there. Just like I was once a broke college student, I was determined not to let that label stick.

Being a starving artist sounds rebel-like, but it's soul killing. I've seen more often than not people who can't create because they haven't eaten in a while or they don't know where they're going to sleep, how to pay their electric bill or care for their kids. There's nothing fun about that kind of uncertainty.

Making a living as an artist is achievable. But to accomplish this, you must understand the business of being a freelancer.

No, it's not cool to read over the terms of a contract to make sure you're not giving away your rights; no, it's not interesting to have a schedule day in and day out so that you make sure you're making the art that will pay the bills. But that's what being a working artist is all about. You're the boss now. You Inc. is in business.

So how can being a starving artist be part of the drama?

Because the mythology can lure you into laziness. If you're not careful, it will become a self-fulfilling prophecy.

How?

By you making excuses. If you don't expect to make a living, then earning only $1000 for your writing in two years, while your boyfriend (spouse, parents etc...) pays for all the expenses, won't bother you. In your mind it's expected. No paying gigs for your band? Oh well, being a musician is hard and only the big acts make a living. If you're not careful, you'll start doing really dangerous things like working for free for exposure that never comes.

If you take nothing else from this book, please remember: If you want to be a working artist get paid for your work.

Don't let people manipulate you and use your skills for their own benefit with the silly promise of no measurable exposure. I mean it. That other photographer is getting paid, so is that writer, and that artist. That musician doesn't even show up unless the price is right. You must put a value on yourself and your work.

Free is a very strategic business option that is an entire book on it's own. For now—get paid.

"Money madness takes many forms. Financial anorexia is one of them.

We refuse to deal with money, so we underearn and underspend.

We get "high" on our lack of money."

— JULIA CAMERON

Money is a good measure.

If you want to be a professional, you have to have a measure. If your income isn't increasing, you need to take a step back and wonder why. Are you undercharging? Are you in the wrong market? If you have no measure, you won't hustle the way you need to. You'll send out five poems and two stories a year and say that you're 'working'. You'll sing the same ten songs you wrote seven years ago and see no need to learn or add more.

You're better than that.

You can make a living as an artist but that means blasting past the starving artist label.

How do you do that?

If you're fortunate enough to get people to support

you, then work your behind off. Write hundreds of stories and don't worry about the avalanche of rejections (either from readers if you indie publish or editors if you go to traditional magazines). Create your own venues to display your art, host your own shows, have your own channels.

Kick the Cinderella myth to the curb and stop waiting for Prince Charming. Get your own damn horse and take yourself where you want to go. Don't wait around for a princess to kiss you and turn you from a frog into a prince.

You may not make a lot of money initially, but you'll be a professional. If you have to take a 'money' job (not to be confused with a career job) to pay the rent, buy food, pay utilities so that you can continue to create, go for it. Having a side job that pays the bills, doesn't make you any less of an artist. The definition of an artist is quite simple—someone who creates art.

HOW TO FORGET THE DRAMA

Stay sober, stay clean, stay healthy. Addiction saps you.

Guard your space. Be careful who you spend time with. As the saying goes 'show me your friends and I'll tell you who you are.' Surround yourself with positive people both online and off.

Read inspiring books, watch inspiring shows.

Be boring.

Develop a routine. Have a set schedule when you create. You don't want to be the gossip story on anyone's lips. You want people to talk about your work—not you.

Use the 'if-then' strategy. Prepare for setbacks or headaches in advance using the 'if-then' approach. "If Y magazine doesn't accept my story, then I'll send it to X magazine." "If I'm working on a painting, then I won't answer the phone." "If I can't work at this time, then I'll work at this time." Having a backup strategy helps you feel more in control.

Think like a scientist. I know the thought of thinking like a rational, left-brain sends shivers through most of you who hated math and Chemistry, but just listen to what I have to say. It is very important not to refer to your projects as 'your babies' because then you may become too attached and make irrational choices. Approach your projects and outcomes in an objective manner.

Take an evidence-based approach. Look at the data of an unfavorable outcome in an objective manner. For example, you didn't get the role? What does that mean? No, it does not mean you're an awful person who will never make it as an actor. When you strip your personal feelings out of the equation, what is really true? Did you perform your best? Did the role suit you? What can you learn from it? How can you apply what you learned to your next audition?

Learn the difference between making a living and building a career. One can be short-term (i.e. two to five years), the other is long-term (ten years plus). Both are fine. You can have a career and not make a living, you can make a living and not build a career or you can do both.

The choice is yours.

Having a life that's drama-free can be a lot of fun and is essential to your long term career, unless you get a little smug and fall into the next trap...

7

FORGET HAVING IT MADE

Okay, so you've sold a bunch of novels. Got picked up by a movie producer. Had your artwork displayed in international galleries. You've got money in the bank and you're supporting yourself.

Think you have it made?

Think it's all rainbows and lollipops from now on?

Sorry, you've got to keep it up.

You've got to keep creating and learning.

Your freedom has a price. It's called uncertainty.

The moment you start 'resting on your laurels' you forget that.

If you want to last a couple of decades—not just a few years, decades—you have to adopt a long term mindset. Many artists have short 5-10 year careers. I didn't really believe that until I started to see a trend among artists (especially in publishing) who've come before and after me. Many of them last five years, a few ten. But they rarely make it to fifteen and twenty.

Why?

For a number of reasons. Some personal—they achieved what they wanted to, they got discouraged, they had a string of hits and then one project bombed and they didn't recover, or they were hot in a market that suddenly cooled.

It's called life.

You will have ups and downs because having a successful career does not shield you from life. That's why so many artists have a hard time after a trend disappears. They thought the money would flow at high numbers forever and didn't prepare for the dip. As a freelance artist, you can't treat your money like a salary, never assume it will always stay at a certain level or (heaven forbid) increase. When it does, great. Plan accordingly. But what do you do when it drops 40-60 %? Handle your money wisely. And you have to handle your greatest asset—your mind—with the same diligence.

. . .

That means plan for the unexpected and also plan for learning.

Keep learning or you may become creatively stale.

You must always be flexible if you want to keep your creativity flowing.

> *"A writer's life is not designed to reassure your mother."*
>
> — RITA MAE BROWN

Creativity shudders and dies under the weight of rigid rules and if you start to believe your own hype (I'm a great artist, I don't need to know that) and let your ego get in the way...well, no one owes you a living, which is key to a professional artist's long-term success.

No matter how high you rise, always strive to do your best. You may fall short sometimes, but that's okay. It's expected. Many artists play it safe. And that's fine if it works, but sometime their audiences start to dwindle and then they wonder why they don't have the career they'd had in the past.

HOW TO FORGET ABOUT HAVING IT MADE

Keep practicing. You don't grow by accident. Just because you do the same thing for years doesn't mean you're improving. Continue to practice and learn the fundamentals in your field.

Strive to top yourself.

Don't confuse action with activity. There's a saying that says, If the devil can't make you bad, he'll make you busy. Running on a treadmill is an activity. Walking to the store to buy something is an action. If you're busy with things that aren't important then soon your life will be filled with little successes that never get you to where you want to be. Take a moment to think about why you're doing something.

What is its real impact?

What do you really need to do to get to the next level?

Keep learning. Get a magazine subscription popular in your industry, attend workshops or sign up to teach them (that's another way to learn).

Realize that setbacks are normal. There's nothing wrong with you if your career hits a rocky patch—you haven't lost your mojo, you're not doomed to failure, your best days aren't behind you.

Many artists let their careers die because they don't know how to bounce back.

A long-term career is not linear it has ups and downs. Don't blame yourself, you're not alone. It happens to all working artists, you just keep moving forward.

Don't slip into the soft rut of 'having it made' and please don't let the next trap fool you...

"The world doesn't reward mediocrity."

— ROBERT HERJAVEC

8
FORGET BEING FOUND

As artists, we've been sold a load of rubbish.

We've been taught that it is important to be found. To be the name that comes up on the top of a list when someone types in something. We focus on promoting our products and despair of not being able to stand out. We complain that it's too crowded, it's too noisy, no one will listen.

And you're absolutely right, if your strategy is all about being picked. If you want to embody the myth of being the beautiful girl discovered in the ice cream parlor (the sleeping princess, the boy with the special scar on his forehead, the chosen one) then you're going to be disappointed. When you're trying to be like everyone else, you're in deep trouble. And you can whine about it all you want. Nobody cares—

except all the *other* people who want to be picked too.

However, if you aim to have a long-term career as a working artist, you can learn from people like actors Sylvester Stallone or Vin Diesel and create your own platform and have people seek you out. That's when life gets interesting.

You don't want to worry about being left on the shelf.

There's no shelf.

And you'll only get lost in the crowd if you're generic and bland.

You want to inspire people so that they'll race out to seek you. You want them to type in *your name* when they're looking for a book, song, podcast etc…

This approach takes the luck factor out of the equation.

Build your unique brand, one story, one performance, one painting at a time, and soon people will come to you. You never go to them. This approach takes time, but it will be time well spent.

Let me share a high school analogy with you—a place I escaped…um graduated from with indescribable joy.

There's a kid who wants to be popular, who's

desperate to be liked and tries hard to please everyone. And then there's another kid who walks into a room with a 'so what?' attitude. The 'this is who I am, take it or leave it' persona.

Guess who commands attention?

The first kid may get attention initially with his eager beaver smile, but it won't last long. The second kid may be ignored at first, but slowly the mystery around her will gain interest and this kid will not have to change to suit whoever she's trying to impress because she's not trying to impress anyone. She's just being herself.

That kind of authenticity matters. It's a longer road, I know, but it's longer-lasting too.

Let your work stand on its own without the gimmicks and hype. Like the 'cool' kid, you say this is who I am, like it or not. I'm not here to please everybody.

"Nice to be found. Essential to be sought."

— SETH GODIN

HOW TO FORGET ABOUT BEING FOUND

Forget about overnight success. It breaks my heart every time I read about a fifteen year old posting on YouTube and bemoaning how hard it is to be discovered because the platform's so crowded. She'll talk about big YouTube stars never once taking into account that that 21-year-old top reviewer spent eight years posting his messages before he made it, that successful comedy act struggled for years before getting notice. If you don't know how long it really takes to be a success in your field, you're in for a load of heartache.

There will always be outliers, but more often than not those big successes you hear about spent years to get to where they are now.

When starting on your journey, or even if you're in the middle, you need to ask yourself if you have what it takes to put in the long hours and *years* of labor to achieve what you want.

How bad do you want it?

How committed are you?

Don't plan on being the exception. There are people who can eat whatever they want and not gain a pound. That's not most people. So it would be really silly for someone to eat whatever they want and gain weight and then complain about it. Don't waste your time trying to fight the norm.

As an artist you're going to be discouraged, dismissed, ignored and feel like giving up. I don't care how pretty you are, someone's going to think you're not pretty enough (Model Heidi Klum was initially told she was 'too short, too heavy...too bosomy'), someone will think you don't even have a right to be in your chosen field (critics of comedian Noah Trevor don't think he's a real comedian).

I don't care if you know of an artist who's never had to audition, who always gets their work accepted into top magazines, who has gallery owners scrambling for his latest work. That likely won't be you. Most artists have to develop a thick skin and strategize in order to have long-term careers—work with that.

Start working on your next project. Staying in the arts is a numbers game. The more you have, the more likely people will take notice. Keep on creating more songs, more comics, performing, showing your work etc...

Infuse your work with your special viewpoint. As Seth Godin said in his book *Purple Cow* remarkable work is work people will remark about. And remember, it doesn't have to be everybody. Just a few and you're on your way. Like James Bonnet said in his book *Stealing Fire from the Gods*,

"...keep in mind that your hardcover book only has to appeal to one in a hundred readers to become a bestseller. That means that ninety-nine out of a hundred potential readers can completely ignore or dislike your work and you can still be a bestselling author."

Change 'readers' and 'author' to whatever suits you.

Don't wait for the limelight, act as if you already have it. Just like desperate, lonely people at a bar hoping to score, your over-eagerness may repel others. Stand tall, create with passion, let whatever you've created go, then start all over again.

If you follow this, then you'll shoot past the next trap without a problem…

9
FORGET CREATING A MASTERPIECE

For some reason, many aspiring artists only focus on one project, as if a lifetime of experience needs to be smashed into one big moment.

Most long-term professionals create a body of work. Think about that.

One book versus fifty.

One song versus hundreds.

One painting versus thousands.

Too often many artists get stuck. They attach themselves to the outcome of what they deem to be their one great project.

They don't send their work out.

They worry about it.

They try to fix it, which usually makes it worse because they don't know what to fix.

They get other people's opinions, which can be creative suicide depending on who you're asking.

They stop themselves.

Three things lead to what I call the 'masterpiece' trap.

Believing in the big moment.

Many artists want that 'before' and 'after' moment. The moment when everything changes. But usually the moment is an accumulation of many insignificant moments. Like a young aspiring rocker at age twelve teaching himself to play the guitar. (David Grohl, of the rock band Foo Fighters). Like the kid dropping out of school and spending the next five years reading all the books in the library (August Wilson, playwright).

Writing your first novel or creating your first album feels big and you can celebrate it, but it's just one moment, hopefully in the line of many. You don't get to decide which moment will take you to the next level. It may be your fifteenth story that gets chosen. Lots of musicians have albums that didn't do well, but in order to be successful they had to continue to create and produce.

Feeling your work must be (or is) important.

Sorry, you don't get to choose which of your creations will hit the big time. So just create your work and let it go. I know you put your passion into your work. I know you put in time and effort and learned your craft and did your best. I know it means a lot to you. Congratulations. But once it's done, let it go.

Get started on the next one.

I mean it.

Finish and send it out, share it.

Fear that if you don't do something amazing it will ruin your reputation.

If you're an aspiring artist you don't have a reputation yet.

If you're already a working artist, relax.

Your reputation will outlast a flop. It's done all the time. So what if you publish a book that nobody buys? So what if no one saw your film? That song that didn't work? Oh well…

A failed project is painful to you, but if you have other projects, it won't matter in the long run. And sometimes those failures turn into victories later on.

Finish the project and send its imperfect behind out into the world and…yes, start on another.

Repeat.

I'm sorry, but you don't get to choose how important your work is. That's not your job. Your job is to create and let your work stand on its own.

HOW TO FORGET ABOUT CREATING A MASTERPIECE

Say you'll create one in, let's say, fifteen to twenty years and just get busy with your current (unimportant) work. Focus on creating a body of work.

Get over yourself. You're making your work too important.

Do what you need to do to express yourself then move on. Some people will disagree with this premise because they believe that all artists must elevate humanity. Fine, let them do it.

But don't argue with them because that will get you into the final trap...

> *"When you sit down to write, tell the truth from one moment to the next and see where it takes you."*
>
> — DAVID MAMET

10
FORGET CHOOSING SIDES

As an artist you don't have to choose.

You get to be many things, so don't lock yourself in with labels. Others will do that for you anyway.

Many long-term working artists combine two vastly different forms. Servant and warrior.

A servant who serves the work.

A warrior who fights the demons of doubt and fear in order to create.

An artist must be both bold and humble.

Bold enough to create their work and share it with the world.

Humble enough to continue to learn and trust that the right people will find their work.

An artist must study their craft yet forget rules that will stop their creativity.

HOW TO FORGET CHOOSING SIDES

Stop looking for traitors and enemies. They have nothing to do with your career and how you decide to structure it.

Don't get caught up in emotional issues. It can blind you to what's really happening in your industry and the opportunities that are there.

Do what feels right for you. There are many sides each with pros and cons. Everyone has varied experiences. That's how life works. As a creative, don't get caught up in taking sides.

Really.

You're better off creating.

The fact that an artist can use a digital pen and tablet to airbrush a painting doesn't stop him from also picking up a paintbrush and doing a landscape.

You're better off creating.

The fact that a musician can go to a studio to record doesn't stop her from creating music at home on her laptop.

You're better off creating and reaching your audience in the way that suits you.

Don't be tethered, float free.

Realize that you have the right to change your mind.

Don't stay on one track just because you started on it.

That's the beauty of a new day and the key to creative freedom.

> *"There are other writers who would persuade you not to go on, that everything is nonsense, that you should kill yourself. They, of course, go on to write another book while you have killed yourself."*
>
> — JOHN GARNER

Whether or not you agree with forgetting about the ten things I've listed doesn't matter.

Just consider a few things: Don't worry about disappointing people, you're going to anyway you might as well do what you want to do.

Be too busy to care.

Be too happy to fight.

Be too smart to engage.

Be you and forget the rest.

Are you an artist?

Forget I asked you that. Show me.

SNEAK PEEK

The Writer Behind the Words

If you enjoyed 10 *Things to Forget: To be Creatively Free*, you may also enjoy *The Writer Behind the Words: Steps to Success in the Writing Life*, available now from your favorite bookseller.

Turn the page for a sample...

DEFINING SUCCESS

Publication is not necessarily a sign of success.

— WILLIAM SLOANE

Setbacks are a part of any creative endeavor, and you'll find plenty of setbacks in the writing life. You'll lose contests, clients, customers (called readers); get nasty reviews, see others succeed before you...and it will hurt.

If you are discouraged to the point that you can't write anymore, I suggest that you stop writing for publication. Write for the joy of it, for personal satisfaction, and not for anyone else. Why? Because publication isn't a cure for anything that ails you and writing doesn't get easier. Stephen King had a cocaine habit after he was published, Grace Metalious, the author of *Peyton Place*, drank herself into the ground, and authors still commit suicide.

So if you're hoping that being published will:

Validate you

Make you worthy

Make you happy

Make you successful

Make you attractive

I'm here to tell you it won't. Writing to get "love" (attention, adoration, etc.) is dangerous because not everyone will like your work. They're not supposed to. Even if you sell a million copies, one nasty review will stick in your mind like gum in your hair. You will need to make the act of writing (the creative process) a joy, a cushion for the pain of the business. Someone else will sell more, make more, and have more. It doesn't matter. Your life has nothing to do with them. Enjoy being a creative person, and write.

For many people, external goals never satisfy the inner spirit. Many people get married, have kids, buy a new car, hoping those things will make them happy. They may not. People win the lottery and still end up miserable. If there's something lacking inside you it will still be lacking after publication. You will need to start defining what success means to you. Don't use someone else's definition. Be truthful to your inner desire and need. Don't judge it. Just listen. It's your desire and it's meant to be heard. Get a journal and write about your ideal life. Getting published is great, but go beyond that. Why?

Consider this:

- You could get a couple of articles published and earn a grand total of two hundred dollars for the next five years. Would you consider yourself successful?
- You could get published and get no byline. Is that success?
- You could be published in mass-market paperback instead of hardcover.
- You could have an article published in a magazine no one has ever heard of.
- You could get a six-figure book deal and never publish again and have your book go out of print within a year.
- You could get 100,000 downloads for your free work and sell only 100 copies of your paid work in the same year.

Define success for yourself. Try to make it something that does not depend on others. For example, success could be:

- *Completing a short story when you've never finished anything before*
- *Making a part time living as a writer*
- *Writing six articles that inform*
- *Editing an anthology*
- *Becoming a career writer of more than ___books, stories or articles*

People put a lot of weight on what a "writer" truly is or is supposed to be and in the process they lose themselves trying to achieve a perceived ideal. A writer writes. That's all. Base your success on that foundation. I'm certain it will go beyond just "Getting published."

DREAMS AND GOALS VERSUS MISSION

Many people confuse dreams, goals and mission. They are very different things. Dreams are wonderful things you strive for but can't control; goals are actions you can control and are destination oriented while missions are usually limitless.

Why do you think Mother Teresa said "More tears are shed over answered prayers than unanswered ones"? Because many people set and achieve goals only to discover that they are still unhappy. The reason is that goals are fleeting and changeable. They are future events that a person can long for and work towards, but once achieved will become something else. Dreams can be something someone wants but is out of their reach because of no fault of their own. A mission is a lasting motto that carries one through life.

For example, getting published by a top known magazine is a dream, you can send your work in but it may never be chosen no matter how many years you try; publishing a book is a goal, it is something you can control if you take the indie route and publish yourself. Being a career writer is a mission, it is a long term motivation. Becoming a lead author at a small press is a dream, being a diligent, reliable, prolific author with a body of work is a mission; getting an award is a goal, being a masterful storyteller is a mission. It's the present moments that give joy. You need dreams to create your goals to help you fulfill your mission. In the end you'll have a solid foundation to carry you through.

Examples of dreams:

Make $100,000 a year

Become a bestselling author on a certain list

Sell 50,000 copies of my book

Examples of Goals:

Write __pages a day

Indie publish six books a year

Send out 30 short stories to paying markets

Example of Missions:

Have a long term career

Educate others

Be a professional, contributing writer

Be physically and mentally healthy

Take the time to create your list of goals and your mission. Remember that a goal has an ending; a mission does not.

THE ONE SECRET EVERY WRITER KNOWS

> *Most writers are in a state of gloom a good deal of the time; they need perpetual reassurance.*
>
> — JOHN HALL WHEELOCK

> *Action is eloquence.*
>
> — WILLIAM SHAKESPEARE

The secret every full-time writer knows is that action is the key to getting what you want. It is the writer's greatest weapon against failure. To achieve this mindset first you have to redefine failure. Failure is not a rejection, a low royalty statement, a book that hits the market and dies or an idea that doesn't work. Failure is stopping your dreams due to circumstance. Failure is receiving one rejection from an editor or the marketplace and never writing again.

> *You may have a fresh start any moment you choose, for this thing we call failure is not the falling down, but the staying down.*
>
> — MARY PICKFORD

Many new writers tell me how discouraged they are. I understand. I also get discouraged. I tell them to keep going, don't stop, you're great etc. They thank me and go back into the writing world safe in their armor of praise. A few weeks or months later, they write again. They receive a rejection or fail to become a finalist in a contest or their latest indie published project didn't sell as well as they'd hoped and they are upset. They bemoan their fate and wail about how unfair the world is and then wait for the expected words of encouragement. But this time I don't provide the same "rah, rah" cheer.

Why? Because in the writing world you have to become your own cheerleader. Most writers fall by the wayside, not due to lack of talent, but due to lack of persistence. Writing is an art and Art (with a capital "A") is bigger than criticism, acceptance, acknowledgement or dismissal.

Art must be created in spite of, not because of. Writing because of something (a trend, a contest, an editor etc.) can be a prison to a writer. Your words have only one master — your spirit, which has an unquenchable curiosity and desire to communicate. Well-meaning people will tell you how to write, what to write, when to write or why you should write, but in the end your spirit is your master.

Notice I didn't say you, because your conscious self

will be too cautious and too clever to write with complete truth. But your spirit is a wild child who sees what you don't and knows what you may not readily admit. It is your free spirit that the world needs. We have enough cautious mask-wearers, we don't need one more in print sounding like everyone else. You must take action.

Action is sending out queries to paying markets, asking for or developing assignments, writing one more story, jotting down ideas. Action is movement, movement creates energy, energy draws success. Most successful writers have more rejections, setbacks and heartbreaks than writers who have stopped writing. Now that you know the secret, try it for yourself. This can be accomplished by taking small or mini steps.

Mini Steps Towards Action

- Buy a pen and paper.
- Open a file called Writing.
- Develop a ritual. One writer I know has to repeat "I'm brilliant" five times before he starts writing.
- Lower your expectations. Just because a bestselling author writes twenty pages a day doesn't mean you have to. Write a

paragraph or a page then congratulate yourself.
- Summarize your idea in a sentence or two.
- Do micro-movements. Read SARK's book *Make Your Creative Dreams Real* (listed in Resources section) to find out how.
- Understand what's truly ahead of you and prepare for setbacks. Read Seth Godin's book *The Dip* (listed in the Resources section)
- Identify writing markets.

USING YOUR GIFTS

Today I looked out the kitchen window of my parents' house and noticed a brown wren. It sat on a railing in their backyard and blended in with the bare trees and dry leaves on the ground. I noticed it, not because it was beautiful, but because it was singing. It sang so loudly that its song echoed through the trees. I stood amazed that something so small could have such a strong voice.

Many of you are just like this wren. You may never be the "blue jay bestseller" or the "eye-catching award-winning cardinal" but your voice will have an impact on those who hear it. So sing — loud and strong.

PREPARING FOR RAIN

Always remember that you're good enough as you are to reach your dreams. I know it's hard to believe, especially in a culture that promotes "self-improvement" for everything from physical shape to career choice, but you don't need to change. In spite of all your imperfections, fears, doubts, and worries, you have everything you need to succeed. How do I know this? Because you're here. You're alive and you're no different from others who have traveled this path before you.

Your job is to speak your intentions and to do them. If you truly want to quit, do it now. Why would a book about resilience talk about quitting? Because if you're discouraged by the rain, then the storm is going to kill you.

Some people scoff and think, "Once I'm published everything will be okay. It's worse being unpublished, ignored, having friends laugh at my dreams, having editors dismiss me, and I'm unhappy. A traditional book or magazine contract, a successful indie project or feature article will at least be an umbrella and then I will be able to deal with the rain."

Yes, publication (both traditional and indie) can be a protection against the rain. I know how hard it is to be unpublished. I was unpublished for years. I know the sting of rejections, the "You're crazy" speech, the dreaded "You've still not published anything?" question, and the "Try something sensible" lecture. Being multi-published allows me to respond to snide comments with a certain wicked delight and conceit that I didn't have before I was published. However, I had confidence before I was published. Although publication is an umbrella, it is not a panacea. Can an umbrella keep you safe in a storm? No. Many indie published writers are discovering this sooner than their traditionally published counterparts. What kinds of storms are out there? Consider these:

- After years you finally sell a book to an editor who loves your work. A few months later, the editor leaves and your new editor hates your voice, your main character and you.
- You realize being an indie publisher doesn't work for you.
- Your literary lawyer decides to become a magician.
- An editor kills your article.
- Reviewers sharpen their swords and publicly slice up your work.
- "Readers" post nasty reviews online.
- The front cover of your book is lousy.
- The back cover blurb of your book is great;

unfortunately it's not what your book is about.
- Sales are low so your publisher drops you.
- Your indie sales are low and your spouse tells you to quit or threatens to leave you.
- You change your name due to low sales and write a different book, which also gets buried in the publishing cemetery.
- The main vendor for your indie published books closes unexpectedly.

Still think publication is safe? If you do, I also suspect you'd try holding onto a twig during a tornado.

Publication is nice, but it won't keep you safe. Life happens. How you respond to the obstacles is the key. Many writers have experienced the above impediments and their careers are doing fine. You can do the same, if you're willing to be honest with yourself about what you can handle. How do you deal with setbacks? If you're like most people, you become desperate and either blame life, work harder and grow frustrated, or throw up your hands and give, up saying "I knew I couldn't do it."

Setbacks are not a reflection of you. Later I'll show you how to handle them, but right now you need to face your temperament and see if it matches your goals.

- Do you want to be a writer or to have written?
- Do you want to play it safe or do you mind taking risks?
- Do you live by ultimatums? "If I don't make it by such and such time, then..."
- Do you expect to succeed?

There are no right answers. You know yourself better than anyone else can know you, but it is critical that you know what you're working toward. One thing I have discovered is that people who succeed think in a way that is different from those who don't succeed. People who succeed usually reflect on the future, while those who fail reflect on the past.

If your five indie published books are not selling do you____?

- Berate yourself for not doing well
- Decide to go traditional

OR

- You continue to write and publish
- Create better covers, blurbs and start on the next book

If you miss a deadline, do you tell yourself_____?

- I'll never succeed because I'm always disorganized

OR

- I missed this deadline because I overbooked. Next time I won't do that.

If you get a rejection do you _____?

- Shrug your shoulders and submit again.

OR

- Decide that you're a loser because you always get rejections?

If you sign a terrible contract, do you _____?

- Berate yourself and think of all the other mistakes you've made.

OR

- Swear, then start to learn how to read a contract better with the help of a literary lawyer?

Do you see the pattern? Winners always look

forward; they learn from their mistakes, but they do not let past behaviors stop them. There is another trait that separates successful writers from unsuccessful writers — Attitude. I'll give you an example of two writers: Felicity and Malcolm. They have the same world experience, same talent and drive, but different attitudes. Both are seeking to be traditionally published.

When Felicity gets a rejection, she sees it as a failure. She thinks of all the other authors who haven't received as many rejections as she has. She knows she's not as good as they are, and hates the fact that she's shy. She knows she could never promote and network the way her critique group says she should. She wonders if she has what it takes to make it.

When Malcolm gets a rejection he sighs, is disappointed, and crosses the name of the editor off his list for that particular project (he may try another project in the future). He knows that marketing is about trial and error and that others have struggled and have ultimately succeeded. He knows that a good product will sell and he doesn't worry that he isn't as outgoing as his friend Randy, who is selling lots of freelance articles. Malcolm knows that there are other writers who are shy, like he is, but who have succeeded. So he keeps on trying.

Felicity and Malcolm are two people with the same

problem, but with different attitudes. Work on your attitude or outlook, but don't be mean to yourself. We all make mistakes on occasion. Virginia Woolf sent out her work without her address and a self-addressed stamped envelope for the editor to reply. Remember that all noted writers were once beginners or unknown mid-list writers. Learn to lighten your load and relax. It's hard to run with shackles.

ALSO AVAILABLE

The Writer Behind The Word: Steps to Success in the Writing Life.

ABOUT THE AUTHOR

Dara Girard is an award-winning, national bestselling author of more than forty books.

She has written numerous articles for *Byline* magazine, *The Writer's Notebook*, *Romance Writers Report*, newsletters and e-zines. She has also interviewed many industry professionals on the Novelists Inc blog.

Visit her website at www.daragirard.com.

You can write her at:

contactdara@daragirard.com

or

Dara Girard

PO Box 10345

Silver Spring, MD 20914

If you would like to receive a reply, please send a self-addressed, stamped envelope.

www.ingramcontent.com/pod-product-compliance
Lightning Source LLC
Chambersburg PA
CBHW050331120526
44592CB00014B/2132